DIESEL
MEMORIES

ROGER SIVITER ARPS

Blue-liveried 'Western' Class No. D1011 *Western Thunderer* takes the Westbury station line at Fairwood Junction with the 10.46 Newton Abbot–Paddington train. The date is 12 July 1969. Completing this Western Region scene is the ex-GWR signal-box and semaphore bracket signal. *(Hugh Ballantyne)*

First published 2010

The History Press
The Mill, Brimscombe Port
Stroud, Gloucestershire, GL5 2QG
www.thehistorypress.co.uk

British Library Cataloguing in Publication Data.
A catalogue record for this book is available from the British Library.

ISBN 978 0 7524 5245 6

Typesetting and origination by The History Press
Printed in Malta
Manufacturing managed by Jellyfish Print Solutions Ltd

Unless otherwise stated, all pictures were taken by
Roger Siviter.

Contents

After the end of steam in 1968, English Electric Class 40 diesels were in regular use on the Crewe to North Wales trains. Prior to 1968, these trains were mainly in the hands of BR Standard Class 5MT 4–6–0s. On a damp Saturday 5 June 1982, Class 40 No. 40008 pulls out of Chester General station with an afternoon Bangor–Crewe train.

This side view of Class 33 No. 33065 was taken on the evening of 29 August 1991 as it climbs the bank out of Sherborne with the 17.38 Exeter St David's–Waterloo train. The Class 33s, which were introduced between 1960 and 1962, were often to be seen on the Waterloo–Exeter route prior to the introduction of the Class 159 turbo units in 1993.

Introduction

The dictionary definition of the word 'memory' is a 'faculty by which things are recalled to or kept in the mind,' and this is certainly the case with railways, for many of us not only recall things from many years ago, but also from the more immediate past.

As with steam traction, which finished on our railways well over forty years ago, diesel memories can now start in the late 1950s, when diesel locomotives gradually took over from steam locomotives, culminating in the end of steam on British Railways in 1968.

Today, many people think of the diesel traction of yesteryear as once they thought of the steam locomotive. Witness the crowds that turn out to see preserved diesels such as Deltics, 'Westerns', 'Peaks', Class 40s, etc. on special charter trains, and also the great interest in 'diesel days' on many of our very fine preserved railway lines. And so I hope that this book will bring back many diesel memories to people. With such a vast subject, this is naturally an overview, with coverage from the late 1950s to about the end of the millennium, with many of the locomotive classes and infrastructure not now to be seen on today's railways.

In compiling this book, I am grateful to Hugh Ballantyne for the use of his fine pictures, my wife Christina for typing the manuscript, my publisher for freedom of layout, and last but not least all the railwaymen who make it all possible.

Roger Siviter ARPS
Teignmouth, 2010

English Electric Class 50 No. 50005 *Collingwood* waits to leave Penzance on the morning of 17 August 1984 with the 09.32 to Paddington. It would arrive in the capital city after the 305☐ mile journey and twelve stops, at 15.29.

Diesel Memories

During Sundays in the mid-1980s, many south–north trains via Birmingham New Street instead of taking the direct route south of Worcester at Abbotswood Junction to Stoke Works Junction (south of Bromsgrove) would run through Worcester and Droitwich to Bromsgrove and then on to New Street station. This meant trains running through Worcester Shrub Hill station, with all its infrastructure and semaphores, etc. On 19 April 1984, Class 47/4 No. 47439 glows in the evening sunshine as it powers its way out of Worcester Shrub Hill station (passing a fine GWR bracket signal) with the diverted (SuO) 13.25 Poole–Newcastle train. These Sunday diversions, of course, applied also to the north–south trains.

For many years, the English Electric Class 37 diesels were the main locomotives used on the West Highland routes from Glasgow to Oban and Fort William, and the extension to Mallaig. This first picture shows No. 37424, complete with West Highland Terrier logo, as it runs through the rugged countryside near Glen Finnan with the 15.50 Mallaig–Fort William train on 30 August 1986.

In this second scene, taken on 19 August 1983, we see one of the early Class 37s, No. 37027 *Loch Eil*, about to pass a fine-looking semaphore signal, complete with North British post, as it pulls out of Tyndrum Upper with the 08.34 Glasgow Queen Street–Fort William train.

The final picture in this West Highland trio shows No. 37408 *Loch Rannoch* leaving Crianlarich with the 12.04 Glasgow Queen Street–Oban train, 27 July 1988. The line on the left leads to Crianlarich lower yard, on which can be seen Class 37 No. 37410 *Aluminium 100* with the afternoon goods train to Oban.

Helsby Junction in Cheshire is the setting for the next four pictures. In this first scene we see Class 25 No. 25078 leaving the Hooton and Birkenhead line and heading towards the Manchester area with a tank train from the Shell refinery at Stanlow on 27 June 1984. On the left is the line from Chester to Manchester. Note the high repeating signals for sighting purposes.

In this second picture, taken on 14 April 1983, Class 25 No. 25051 heads through the attractive Dutch-style station with a North Wales–Manchester goods train.

The other two pictures in this quartet were taken just west of Helsby Junction and show, first of all, Class 47/4 No. 47577 *Benjamin Gimbert GC* with a Manchester–North Wales train on the afternoon of 14 April 1983, and on the following day (15 April) we see an eastbound goods hauled by Class 47 No. 47018 and a westbound passenger train hauled by Class 47/4 No. 47540. The Brush Type 4 Class 47 locomotives were built between 1962 and 1967, and at one time were to be found all over the BR system. In both pictures can be seen fine-looking semaphore signals, two of them with lattice posts.

Above: Several examples of this popular class have been preserved, including D9000 *Royal Scots Grey*, now back in two-tone green livery. No. D9000 is seen climbing Rattery Bank out of Totnes with 'The Eastern Envoy' from Reading to Par on 15 May 1999. This is one of the few occasions that Deltics have appeared in the South-West.

Opposite, top: The English Electric Type 5 Deltic locomotives were first introduced in 1961, and with 3300bhp were the most powerful diesel locomotives on the BR system. They were built to replace the LNER Pacific locomotives on the East Coast Main Line (ECML) between London King's Cross and Edinburgh. No. D9004 *Queen's Own Highlander* in the original two-tone green livery is photographed at Escrick, some 7 miles south of York, with an afternoon King's Cross–Edinburgh train, on Sunday 1 May 1966.

Opposite, bottom: By January 1982, the Deltics were withdrawn from service. In the months leading up to this date, they appeared on several special trains, including on 24 October 1981 a York–Aberdeen special – 'The Deltic Salute' – seen here about to leave York station, hauled by No. 55015 *Tulyar*. Note the BR blue livery.

These next two photographs were taken at St Austell on the afternoon of 31 August 1984, when locomotive trains were commonplace throughout the South-West, and indeed throughout most of the country. The first scene shows Class 50 No. 50040 *Centurion* just about to leave the attractive ex-GWR station with the 09.36 Liverpool Lime Street–Penzance train.

Some two hours later at 18.31, and we see 'Peak' Class 45 No. 45005 leaving with the 09.22 Newcastle–Penzance train. Note in both pictures the car park on the left-hand side where the Motorail carriage sidings once were. (See picture on pages 24 and 25).

Above: With the Westbury white horse still prominent, we see English Electric Class 37 No. 37431 *Sir Powys/County of Powys* approaching Fairwood Junction from Westbury station with the 16.54 Bristol–Weymouth train on 16 June 1988. On the right-hand side is the Westbury avoiding line.

Opposite, top: A pair of 'Warship' Class hydraulic diesel locomotives take the line to Westbury at Fairwood Junction with the 06.10 Penzance–Paddington train on 12 July 1969. The locomotives are No. D870 *Zulu* and No. D869 *Zest*. Both are in maroon livery, but with patched or pitted paintwork. These Type 4 locomotives were first introduced in 1960, D870 and D869 (the last two members of the class) being built at Swindon. *(Hugh Ballantyne)*

Opposite, bottom: Turning around from the previous picture, and we see 'Western' Class No. 1052 *Western Viceroy* approaching Fairwood Junction off the Westbury avoiding line with an unidentified Down late morning Paddington–West of England express on 19 August 1972. The lines to and from Westbury station can be seen on the left-hand side. Note also, in the top right-hand corner, the Westbury white horse carved into the chalk hillside of Bratton Down. *(Hugh Ballantyne)*

Class 40 No. 40195 approaches the Birmingham suburb of King's Norton on the Birmingham–Bristol main line with the 'Solent Explorer' bound for Eastleigh open day on 29 May 1983. The Camp Hill relief line is coming in on the right-hand side of the picture. This is mainly used for freight traffic, but with the occasional passenger workings on busy summer Saturdays.

Another Midlands scene, this time at Leicester. On 15 June 1983, Class 31/4 No. 31417 approaches Leicester London Road station with the 07.40 Norwich–Birmingham New Street train. Note the Midland Railway signal-box and the variety of semaphore signals to be seen in this area at this time. By 1988, with resignalling between Leicester and Loughborough, scenes like this would disappear.

The lovely old GWR station at Hagley on the Stourbridge Junction–Droitwich and Worcester line plays host to Class 37 No. 37253 as it runs through on the afternoon of 8 March 1983 with the 12.45 Bescot (Walsall)–Gloucester goods train.

Water Orton, the junction for the Birmingham–Derby and the Birmingham–Leicester routes, sees a pair of English Electric Type 1 Class 20 locomotives Nos 20021 and 20020 as they pass the old signal-box (then used as a tool store, but now gone) with an afternoon breakdown train for the Leicester area. The Class 20s, or 'Choppers' as they are nicknamed because of their engine sound, were introduced between 1957 and 1968 and built either at English Electric Vulcan Foundry, Newton-le-Willows, or by Robert Stephenson & Hawthorn, Darlington. Note the disc indicators, common only to Nos 20001–128; Nos 20129–228 were built with four-character headcode panels. Above the bridge can be seen the attractive entrance to Water Orton station, a typical Midland Railway design.

Above: The Birmingham Railway Carriage & Wagon Company Type 3 locomotives, now Class 33s, were introduced in 1960 and have long been associated with the Southern Region, on both main line and secondary line duties, as these next three pictures bear witness. This first picture, taken on 2 July 1967 at Basing, just east of Basingstoke, shows an unidentified member of the class (then numbered D6500 onwards) with a Down West of England train.

Opposite, top: The next scene, taken on 30 August 1983, sees Class 33 No. 33119 entering East Grinstead station with the empty coaching stock (ECS) for the 18.46 service to London Bridge, having earlier arrived on the 17.34 train from London Bridge station.

Opposite, bottom: In the final picture, taken on 31 August 1983, we see Class 33 No. 33058 at Uckfield station on the 19.10 service to East Croydon (prior to reversing onto the Up platform). The East Grinstead signal-box and Uckfield station buildings date from LB&SCR days, and the semaphore signals are of Southern Railway design.

On 24 July 1982, Class 37 No. 37228 runs past Thornhill LNWR junction at Ravensthorpe (West Riding). The train, which is the 09.28 from Sheffield to Blackpool, is coming off the line from Healey Mills, a route which by that time saw few locomotive-hauled passenger trains. *(Hugh Ballantyne)*

This next picture was taken on the 'Diggle Route' from Huddersfield to Manchester, also on 24 July 1982. Class 25 No. 25158 is seen climbing up to Standedge tunnel near Marsden with the 12.00 Scarborough–Liverpool train. *(Hugh Ballantyne)*

Our next location is Burton Salmon where, on 24 May 1981, Class 31 No. 31175 heads north towards York with an afternoon train from the Sheffield area. These Type 2 locomotives were built by Brush Traction, Loughborough, between 1957 and 1962. Burton Salmon is the junction for the lines from Sheffield to the south and from Normanton to the west. Note also the LNER bracket signal, behind which can just be seen the GNR signal-box which controls the junction.

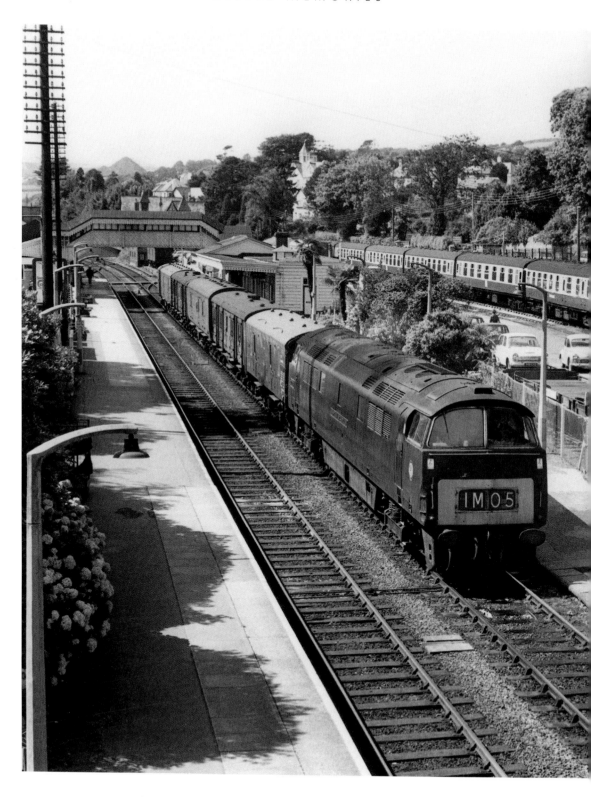

This picture was taken over forty years ago on 8 August 1968, a few days before the end of steam traction on British Railways. 'Western' Class No. D1038 *Western Sovereign*, still in maroon livery despite the advent of the BR blue livery, pulls out of St Austell station at around 2.00 p.m. with the midday Penzance–Plymouth parcels train. On the right-hand side are the Motorail sidings where another unidentified 'Western' Class locomotive, also in maroon livery but with full yellow ends, waits to leave for Kensington Olympia with a Motorail train. The car transporter train finished running in the mid-1980s. Note also the GWR bracket signals, station buildings and fine-looking footbridge. Also, in the background can be seen the 'Cornish Alps' – china clay mounds.

On the former LNWR/LMS North Wales route between Chester and Holyhead, among the many photogenic areas, the line runs round the medieval Conwy Castle. This photograph, taken on a sunny 28 May 1997, shows Class 37/4 No. 37418 *East Lancashire Railway* in EWS maroon livery as it runs by Conwy Castle with the 14.18 Crewe–Bangor train. This high viewpoint is taken from the adjacent field.

The second scene, also captured on 28 May 1997, shows No. 37425 *Sir Robert McAlpine/Concrete Bob* in the Regional Railways livery with the 13.18 Crewe–Bangor service. Dominating both pictures is the fine-looking castle.

Taken on 1 June 1994, this photograph shows No. 37408 *Loch Rannoch* about to thread through the walls of Conwy Castle as it approaches Conwy station with the 14.24 Crewe–Holyhead train.

Prior to the electrification of the area in the early 1990s, Ely had a fine selection of semaphore signals, etc. On the morning of 23 July 1983, Class 31/4 No. 31423 approaches Ely station with the 10.08 Cambridge–Peterborough train. As well as the LNER signal-box, there is a fine display of LNER signals to be seen.

This next picture, taken at Ely seven years later on 10 August 1990, just prior to electrification, shows that the signal-box has now gone, together with several of the semaphore signals. Approaching the camera is a northbound evening freight with Class 37/7 No. 37714 in charge.

Another area famous for its semaphore signalling (which it still has) is Skegness. Class 47 No. 47385 is seen reversing past the fine-looking GNR signal-box with the ECS of the 06.30 Sheffield–Skegness train, which will later form the 10.38 Skegness–Sheffield service. The date is Saturday 4 August 1990.

Havenhouse station on the Skegness–Boston line is the location as the 15.17 Skegness–Nottingham train – formed of two sets of DMUs, the front units being a Craven Class 105 two-car unit – beats a tattoo on the crossing as it hurries westwards on Saturday 16 July 1983. Protecting the crossing are two fine examples of GNR somersault signals, with concrete posts. Completing the scene is the GNR signal-box.

Brush Type 4 No. D1853 approaches Scout Green 'box as it descends Shap bank (Westmorland) with the Up 'Midday Scot' from Glasgow Central to London Euston, on the afternoon of 29 March 1966

Another Brush Type 4 locomotive (this time in the later numbering) No. 47509 *Albion* approaches Bolton station with the 10.43 Nottingham–Glasgow/Edinburgh train on 11 July 1984. This train will divide at Carstairs Junction, with the Edinburgh portion leaving from there at 16.31, followed by the Glasgow section at 16.33.

This picture was taken on 6 June 1968 at Low Barn, near Hoghton, on the Preston–Blackburn line. The Preston–Blackburn van train is hauled by Type 2 Sulzer diesel No. D7651 – later Class 25/3 No. 25301. This class of diesel was first introduced in 1961.

In the late 1980s and through to the early 1990s, the Manchester–Barrow-in-Furness trains were in the hands of the Type 2 Brush Class 31 diesels. On a fine summer morning (26 July 1990) No. 31463 leaves Grange-over-Sands station behind as it heads over the causeway towards Carnforth with the 09.08 Barrow–Manchester service, due to arrive at Manchester Victoria station at 11.24.

English Electric Deltic Class No. 55016 *Gordon Highlander* is framed by the North Eastern signal-box at Selby swing bridge as it approaches Selby station on 24 May 1981 with the 11.43 York–London King's Cross train. At this time, the ECML ran through Selby, but by the mid-1980s the ECML was diverted from the town, thus avoiding the bottleneck where the busy Leeds–Hull line runs through.

Class 47/3 No. 47309 enters Perth station on the line from Dundee with an Up Freightliner train on 1 April 1986. Note the attractive station canopies and pillars, etc.

The Type 3 Beyer Peacock 'Hymek' hydraulic diesels were first introduced in 1961 on the Western Region. With the introduction of BR's Rationalisation policy, withdrawal of the class started in 1971 and was completed in 1975. However, several examples remain in preservation. 'Hymek' No. D7026 is seen arriving at Williton on 18 July 1970 with the 06.20 (SO) Oxford–Minehead train. The Taunton–Minehead branch was closed in January 1971 (Williton being a station on the line), but was later preserved between Bishops Lydeard and Minehead, and is known as the West Somerset Railway, where two members of the 'Hymek' Class are also preserved. *(Hugh Ballantyne)*

Not long after it was built, 'Hymek' No. D7000 passes through Bathampton with the 08.10 Bristol–Portsmouth train on 29 July 1961. *(Hugh Ballantyne)*

Like the 'Hymeks', the 'Warship' class of hydraulic diesels had a fairly short life from 1958 to 1972. 'Warship' No. D803 *Albion* passes Narroways Junction, Stapleton Road, as it climbs out of the city of Bristol with the 12.35 Malago Vale–Old Oak Common van train on 18 May 1969. *(Hugh Ballantyne)*

On 2 August 1960, No. D800 *Sir Brian Robertson* swings round the curves of Shaldon Bridge, Teignmouth, with the 07.30 Penzance–Manchester train. *(Hugh Ballantyne)*

Class 31 No. 31171, plus brake van, runs through Langley Green station on the Birmingham–
Stourbridge Junction line and heads eastwards to Rood End sidings (around half a mile from this
location) to shunt the sidings by Albright & Wilsons chemical works. The date of this wintry scene is
25 January 1984. *(Hugh Ballantyne)*

Another Class 31 in the snow, this time No. 31132. The 'Slug' (as they are sometimes nicknamed
because of their relatively slow power build up) is seen approaching Droitwich Spa station on
16 January 1985 with a Birmingham–Worcester parcels van running via Bromsgrove. In the
background a DMU heads towards Kidderminster with a local service from Worcester.

On 3 March 1995, Class 47 No. 47834 *Fire Fly*, with No. 47835 *Windsor Castle* at the rear of the train, heads north at Stoke Prior, just south of Bromsgrove, with the empty coaching stock of the Royal Train from Gloucester.

'Peak' Class 45 No. 45068 runs light engine through Rowley Regis and heads westwards towards Stourbridge Junction on 25 January 1984. The Class 45s were first introduced in 1959 and throughout the years have worked over most of the BR system. They were called the 'Peak' class because the first members of the class were named after famous mountains, i.e. No. D1 *Scafell Pike*, No. D4 *Great Gable*, etc.

These next three pictures were taken when signal-boxes and semaphore signals controlled train movements around the sea wall between Dawlish and Teignmouth. Here, Class 50 No. 50025 *Invincible* runs by the sea wall and approaches Teignmouth with the 07.00 Oxford–Paignton train on Saturday 28 May 1984.

The signal-box at Dawlish station is still in place today but now out of use. This was not the case on Saturday 30 July 1983, as Class 47 No. 47232 passes by the GWR signal-box with the 07.28 Leeds–Paignton train.

On Saturday 7 July 1984, the Down Motorail train from Paddington to St Austell approaches Teignmouth with Class 47 No. 47091 in charge. From 1982 onwards, the carriages were removed from this train, passengers travelling separately by the normal service train.

Battledown flyover near Worting Junction, just west of the Hampshire town of Basingstoke, is our next location. On Saturday 20 April 1991, Class 47/3 No. 47317 *Willesden Yard* heads towards Southampton with a morning Freightliner train. The lines to and from Salisbury can just be seen running under the girder bridge which carries the line from Southampton. Note the neat-looking metal BR symbol on the locomotive cabside.

The Type 2 Class 27s were still to be found on Edinburgh–Dundee local passenger trains in the early 1980s, as these next three pictures well illustrate. These popular locomotives were first introduced in 1961 and built by BRC&W. They were a development of the earlier Class 26 locomotives and were withdrawn by the late 1980s; however, four locomotives remain in preservation. The first scene shows No. 27036 leaving the western end of Edinburgh Waverley station with an early evening train to Dundee on 10 May 1983. It has just passed Class 47/7 No. 47710 *Sir Walter Scott*, one of the twelve members of the class modified for push-pull operation. An HST and two DMU units complete this busy scene.

On 11 May 1983, No. 27008 heads through the rock cutting at North Queensferry with a midday Dundee–Edinburgh train.

The final view, also taken on 11 May 1983, shows Class 27 No. 27036 leaving the Mound tunnel and running through Princes Street Gardens, Edinburgh, with an afternoon Edinburgh–Dundee train.

This picture was taken in the 1950s at Platform 9 on the Midland side of Birmingham New Street station. A Derby-built DMU waits to leave with an early evening 'rush hour' train to Castle Bromwich in the Birmingham eastern suburbs. With the West Coast electrification scheme, New Street was completely rebuilt in the mid-1960s. *(Roger Siviter Collection)*

Still in Birmingham, but this time on the Western Region at Tyseley Junction, on 31 January 1966. Class 47 Brush Type 4 No. D1853 runs past the signal-box with a Down afternoon express from Paddington.

Another Brush Type 4 (Class 47) hurries through Tyseley Junction (also on 31 January 1966) with a Wolverhampton/Birmingham–Paddington train.

The final scene at Tyseley on 31 January 1966 shows Brush Type 4 No. D1813 coming off the North Warwickshire line from Stratford-upon-Avon with an empty coaching stock train. The junction is obviously still there today but, alas, the signal-box and semaphore signals had disappeared by about 1970.

A Gloucester RC&W Co. Class 119 three-car cross-country DMU departs from Castle
Cary station with the 17.44 train to Weymouth (16.20 ex-Bristol). These units were first
introduced in 1958. Framing this scene, taken on 7 May 1984, are two fine examples of
GWR semaphore signals, the one on the right being a GWR backing signal, complete
with route indicator. The line to Weymouth can be seen veering left in front of the train,
with the former GWR West of England line running off to the right.

An LNER bracket signal (albeit with one arm now missing) frames a three-car DMU at Reedham Junction on 11 August 1990. The train is the 14.50 Norwich–Lowestoft service.

Long Marton viaduct, on the former Midland Railway Settle–Carlisle route, is the location as English Electric Class 40 No. 40082 heads towards Carlisle with a return afternoon pickup freight from the Cumbrian (formerly Westmorland) town of Appleby, which among many things is famous for its jazz festival, on 24 April 1984. The Type 4 Class 40s first appeared in 1958 when several of the class were named after ocean liners. Because of their distinctive engine sound, they are popularly known as 'Whistlers'. They were withdrawn from service by the mid-1980s, but several examples have been preserved.

On 29 September 1983, Class 45/1 No. 45126 approaches Kirkby Stephen (on the S&C route) with the 16.40 Carlisle–Leeds train. Note the high semaphore signals, for sighting purposes.

After the withdrawal from service of the Class 45s in the late 1980s, their duties on the S&C route were mainly taken for the next few years by the Class 31s. Class 31/4 No. 31404 approaches Garsdale on 21 July 1990 with the 10.47 Leeds–Carlisle train. The location is near the site of Garsdale water troughs, the highest in the country. In the background is Dent Dale.

Pinmore viaduct on the Stranraer–Glasgow route in south Ayrshire is regarded as one of the finest in Scotland. On 29 July 1988, Class 37 No. 37031, complete with split headcode panels, runs over Pinmore viaduct with a Stranraer–Glasgow Speedlink freight service.

Just to the south of Montrose, where the Dundee–Aberdeen line crosses the Montrose basin (which runs out into the North Sea), there are two viaducts. On the evening of 2 August 1990, Class 26 No. 26010 heads across the southernmost of the two viaducts with the 17.12 Dundee–Montrose local train, returning to Dundee as the 18.08 ex-Montrose. The Type 2 Class locomotives were first introduced in 1958 and were built by BRC&W at their Smethwick works. They were withdrawn by the early 1990s, but like the Class 27s (which were a development of the Class 26s), many examples survive in preservation.

Regular locomotive-hauled trains on the Far North Line from Inverness to Wick and Thurso ended in 1989. From the early 1980s, Class 37s were to be found in charge of these trains. On 29 August 1986, Class 37/4 No. 37414 crosses over Invershin bridge (south of Lairg) with the 11.35 Inverness–Wick and Thurso train.

We end this quartet of Scottish viaducts with a picture on the Perth–Inverness Highland Main Line. Class 47/4 No. 47630 crosses over Slochd viaduct (north of Aviemore) with the 12.17 Inverness–Edinburgh train on 31 July 1990.

On 5 August 1959, 'Warship' Class No. D801 *Vanguard* leaves Churston on the Kingswear line with the Up 'Torbay Express' to Paddington. In the Brixham bay platform is ex-GWR Class 1400 0–4–2T No. 1470 with the 11.40 train to Brixham. During our family holidays in the late 1940s and early 1950s, I spent many happy hours trainspotting and taking the odd picture at this station. *(Hugh Ballantyne)*

Some fourteen years later than the previous picture, by then the Paignton–Kingswear line had been closed (in 1972) and then reopened as a preserved line (in 1973). In Paignton carriage sidings on 22 July 1973 is 'Western' Class No. D1026 *Western Centurion* waiting to take out a return 'Summer Saturday' train, while in the background can be seen LNER Pacific No. 4472 *Flying Scotsman* and GWR Class 4500 No. 4588 on an early evening special train to Kingswear.

On 8 August 1968, an unidentified maroon-liveried 'Western' Class diesel stands in the car transporter sidings at St Austell with the ECS of the car transporter train, while a Type 2 diesel is seen at the head of the car transporter wagons.

The popular English Electric Class 50 locomotives were built in 1967 and 1968, and in the late 1970s and throughout the 1980s, as well as working on trains to the South-West, were to be found on the Paddington–Birmingham route. This first picture shows No. 50016 *Barham* approaching Aynho Junction, to the south of Banbury, with the 10.09 Birmingham New Street–Paddington train on 21 January 1984.

On a wintry 16 February 1983, we see recently refurbished, but still in the old BR blue livery, Class 50 No. 50014 *Warspite* as it heads south near Lapworth with the 12.38 Birmingham New Street–Paddington train. This location was part of the ex-GWR original four-track section from Birmingham to Lapworth.

Here we see No. 50026 *Indomitable*, now in Network South East livery, as it runs through Harbury cutting (north of Banbury) on 27 May 1989. The train is the 11.18 Wolverhampton–Paddington service.

English Electric Deltic Class No. 50022
Royal Scots Grey passes the 'London 350 Miles'
sign at Houndwood on 27 August 1978 with
the 12.10 Edinburgh Waverley–London King's
Cross train. No. 50022 was numbered first
of the Deltic Class and originally numbered
D9000, but was delivered from the English
Electric's Vulcan Works at Newton-le-Willows,
Lancashire, second after D9001, in the early part
of 1961, the rest of the class following in the
next 15 months. Their original livery was two-
tone green but this was gradually changed to
BR blue from 1966 onwards. *(Hugh Ballantyne)*

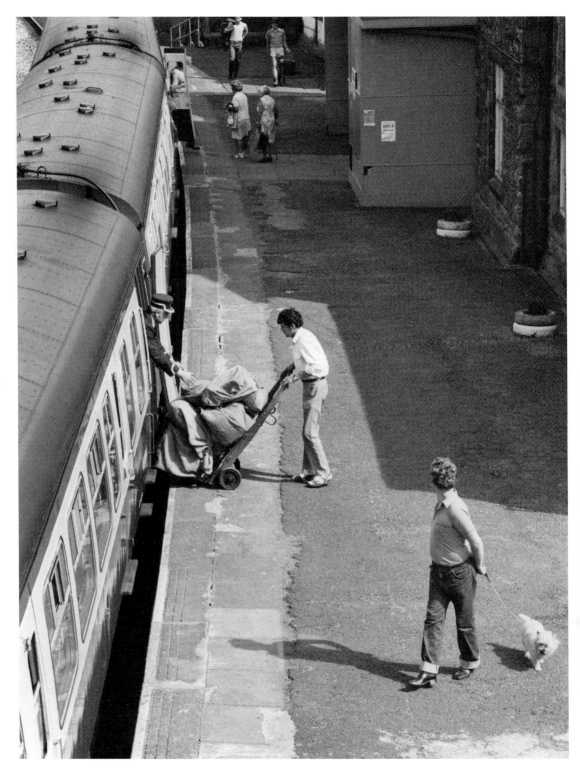

Loading the mail, Mid-Wales style. On 12 August 1983, a Class 101 three-car DMU pauses at Knighton station with the 12.27 train from Swansea to Shrewsbury. Note the guard's smart BR uniform. The Class 101 units date back to the late 1950s and were built by Metropolitan Cammell.

Another Welsh scene, this time at Carmarthen in West Wales. Approaching the station on 20 December 1985 is Class 47/4 No. 47593 *Galloway Princess* with the 07.45 Cardiff–Milford Haven train. This will then be taken forward to Milford Haven from Camarthen at 09.49 by Class 47/4 No. 47575, seen waiting in the loop line on the right-hand side. Carmarthen station has long been a terminus station, the line heading north to Lampeter and Aberystwyth having been closed by 1973.

For many years, the Shrewsbury–Aberystwyth and Pwllheli trains were in the hands of the Class 25 locomotives. These would often work in pairs, as on 13 August 1983, when Nos 25083 and 25076 are caught by the camera as they approach the former Cambrian Railway station at Caersws with the 12.00 (SO) Birmingham–Aberystwyth train. Note the goods shed and semaphore signals and the station signal-box which controls the level crossing.

Until 1986, when the area was resignalled, Inverness was famous for its splendid array of semaphore signals and signal-boxes. On 30 August 1986, Class 37/4 No. 37418 approaches Rose Street Junction, Inverness, with the 10.10 train from Wick, having just passed the fine-looking bracket signal, which still had its Highland Railway posts and finials.

The second Inverness scene, taken on 3 April 1986, shows Class 47/4 No. 47467 passing under one of the two gantry signals by or near Welsh's Bridge signal-box with the 15.40 train from Aberdeen. The signal-box is of Highland Railway design.

Another area famous for its semaphore signals and signal-boxes is Stirling, where on 1 August 1990 Class 26 No. 26040 is seen heading past Stirling Middle signal-box (Caledonian Railway design) with a southbound mixed goods train.

On 31 March 1986, Class 47/4 No. 47551 pulls out of Stirling station with the 13.34 Perth–Glasgow Queen Street train. Framing the train is a fine display of semaphore signals.

An unidentified Class 47 departs from Norwich Thorpe station with the 10.17 (SuO) to London Liverpool Street station on 17 July 1983. Within a short time, due to electrification of the area, the semaphore signals (mostly LNER) would disappear.

Another East Anglian scene, this time at Yarmouth Vauxhall station. Framed by the LNER signal-box and bracket signal, Class 47/4 No. 47543 enters the station on the morning of Saturday 11 August 1990 with the empty coaching stock for the 09.15 Yarmouth–London Liverpool Street train.

A brand new Blue Pullman set stands at Cardiff General station on Friday 8 September 1961, before making a test run towards Newport prior to starting the Paddington–Swansea Blue Pullman service on the following Monday (11 September 1961). (*Hugh Ballantyne*)

Another of the Western Region Pullman sets, this time climbing Hatton bank on 25 July 1966 with the Paddington–Wolverhampton Pullman service. These Western Region sets were built in Birmingham by Metro-Cammell in 1960, but had a short life of just twelve years.

The final BR Blue Pullman picture shows two six-car sets arriving at Bath on 13 June 1969 with the 17.40 Paddington–Bristol Pullman service. *(Hugh Ballantyne)*

The famous 'Brighton Belle' Pullman Car service, which ran three times each way daily between London Victoria and Brighton, is seen near Quarry tunnel, Mersham, heading south to Brighton with the 12.45 from Victoria on 21 March 1972. *(Hugh Ballantyne)*

The English Electric Class 50 locomotives were the mainstay of the Waterloo–Exeter route in the 1980s and early 1990s, as these next three pictures show. First, No. 50017 *Royal Oak* forges its way up the 1 in 37 bank between Exeter St David's and Exeter Central station with the 09.45 service from Exeter to Waterloo, on 16 August 1991. Always famous for the terrific noise they could make, this occasion was no exception!

On 25 July 1984, No. 50011 *Centurion* descends the 1 in 37 bank and approaches Exeter St David's station with the 10.40 service from London Waterloo. Note the GWR signal-box which, with resignalling in the area, would disappear in a few months, but happily was preserved at Crewe Heritage Centre.

The final scene shows No. 50010 *Monarch* as it enters Exeter Central station with the 13.10 Waterloo–Exeter train on 2 April 1988. Note the typical Southern Railway footbridge, which also leads to the New North Road entrance to the station.

Above: On 19 February 1983, Class 40 No. 40012 departs from Hereford station with the northbound 'Welsh Marches Express' from Abergavenny to Shrewsbury, the lower section from Abergavenny to Hereford having been hauled by GWR 'Hall' 4–6–0 No. 4930 *Hagley Hall*.

Opposite, top: For many years, the Class 40 locomotives were to be found on the Aberdeen–Edinburgh trains. An unidentified member of the class runs through the sylvan setting of Edinburgh's Princes Street Gardens as it approaches Waverley station on the afternoon of Sunday 19 June 1966 with an express from Aberdeen. Overlooking the scene is the impressive Caledonian Hotel, behind which Princes Street station used to be located. This station closed in 1965.

Opposite, bottom: Class 40s were also to be found on the Furness line (Carnforth–Barrow) right up to their withdrawal in the mid-1980s. On 22 August 1978, Class 40 No. 40172 heads through the picturesque station at Grange-over-Sands with a southbound midday tank train.

Part of the freight-only line from Walsall (Bescot) to Stourbridge Junction, this being the section from Walsall to Brierley Hill, closed on 19 March 1993. On that day, Class 31 No. 31155 glows in the late afternoon sunshine as it leaves the Wednesbury steel terminal at Potters Lane with a freight working for Bescot.

A short while before the previous picture, and we see Class 47 No. 47238 *Bescot Yard* heading through Potters Lane at Wednesbury with a Round Oak (Brierley Hill) to Bescot trip working, with the headboard 'The Dudley Dasher Memorial Special'. In the right-hand corner can be seen the lines to Wednesbury steel terminal.

This picture was taken on the morning of the last day (19 March 1993) on this Black Country route. The location is Eagle Crossing at Great Bridge, between Wednesbury and Dudley, and shows Class 37/7 No. 37884 *Gartcosh* with a train of steel coils from Bescot to Stourbridge Junction.

An earlier picture on the Bescot–Brierley Hill line, taken on 4 May 1983, shows Class 37 No. 37265 approaching Round Oak (Brierley Hill) with a midday Bescot–Gloucester coal train, with a single-car DMU and two coaches at the rear of the train.

The former Midland Railway route from Settle to Carlisle is renowned for its magnificent scenery and splendid viaducts, none more so than Smardale viaduct, just to the north of Kirkby Stephen. This 12-span 237yd-long viaduct crosses Scandal Beck, as well as the trackbed of the former North Eastern line from Kirkby Stephen (NE) to Tebay on the WCML. On 8 September 1990, Class 31/4 No. 31460 crosses over the graceful viaduct with the 10.47 Leeds–Carlisle train.

At one time, the popular English Electric Class 37 locomotives were to be found all over the BR system, as these next two pictures illustrate. The first scene shows No. 37140 running light engine into Ipswich station on 5 August 1983 in order to take out the 16.20 train to London Liverpool Street. The interesting looking home, distant and shunting signal is of LNER origin.

In the second picture we see Class 37 No. 37181 leaving the Moorswater branch and approaching Coombe Junction (on the Looe branch) with a train of tented china clay wagons for Liskeard and Par on a very damp 4 April 1985. In the background can be seen part of the Moorswater viaduct which carries the WR main line from Plymouth to Penzance.

North British Class D6300 No. 6342 arrives at Cheddar station on 17 August 1963 with the 10.49 (SO) Witham–Yatton train. These Type 2 hydraulic locomotives were first introduced in 1959, and the last few members of the class were withdrawn in 1972. Worthy of note is the fine-looking GWR station, complete with overall roof. *(Hugh Ballantyne)*

Blue-liveried 'Warship' Class diesel No. 810 *Cockade* nears Oldfield Park with train number 8070, the 08.15 Hither Green–Severn Tunnel Junction goods train, on 5 September 1970. *(Hugh Ballantyne)*

One of the popular 'Western' Class diesel hydraulics, No. D1048 *Western Lady*, runs past the site of Southam Road & Harbury station with a midday Birmingham–Paddington train on 17 April 1976. These Type 4 locomotives were first introduced in 1961 and withdrawn from service by 1977, No. D1048 being the last to be withdrawn in February 1977. Happily, No. D1048 is preserved, along with several members of the class, including No. D1015 *Western Champion*, which sees work on main line charter trains.

Type 3 Beyer Peacock ('Hymek') hydraulic diesel No. D7006 leaves Bath Spa station with the 08.10 Bristol–Salisbury train on a cold but bright 4 November 1961. *(Hugh Ballantyne)*

The next three scenes were photographed in the North-East in 1986, prior to the completion of the electrification of the East Coast Main Line (ECML) by the following year. In the first picture, taken on 11 August, Class 47/4 No. 47544 runs through Newcastle city centre, so to speak, with an empty stock train for Newcastle Central station, which will form the 16.17 Newcastle–Liverpool train. The great variety of city buildings, from old to new, makes fascinating patterns.

On 13 August 1986, Class 47/4 No. 47403 *The Geordie* departs from the historic station at Darlington with the 11.24 Newcastle–Liverpool train.

The final picture in this trio was taken on 11 August 1986 at Newcastle Central station. Class 47/4 No. 47544 stands in the centre road as 'Peak' Class 45/1 No. 45135 *3rd Carabinier* waits to leave on the 14.19 service to Liverpool, although looking at the station clocks on the left-hand side, this looks like a late start for this train.

On the evening of 9 August 1984, Class 50 No. 50036 *Victorious* draws into platform 3 at Par
station with the 18.10 train from Newquay, going forward as the 19.08 Par–Plymouth service.
It had earlier worked to Newquay with the 16.20 train from Plymouth. The St Blazey and
Newquay line can be seen swinging to the right at the rear of the train. Note the semaphore
signals and fine-looking GWR station buildings. Also in the background can be seen the
English China Clay complex.

Class 50s were often to be found on summer Saturday trains to Newquay, both from the
Midlands and from London. On Saturday 22 August 1987, No. 50032 *Courageous* approaches
Luxulyan on the Par–Newquay branch with the 09.18 train from Birmingham New Street to
Newquay. With the rationalisation of Newquay station in late 1987 leaving only a single track
in the station, that year would be the final year for locomotive-hauled trains to Newquay, apart
from special charter trains with locomotives at either end to enable 'top and tail' working.

The 16.05 Newquay–Plymouth runs through the Luxulyan Valley on 11 August 1984 with Class 50 No. 50034 *Furious* in charge. This photograph was taken from Treffry aqueduct/ viaduct.

Above: Class 37 No. 37261 once again, this time running through very pleasant scenery near Leith Hall (west of Kennethmont) with an afternoon mixed goods train from Elgin to Aberdeen on 30 May 1990.

Opposite, top: The Inverness–Aberdeen line still saw a fair amount of freight traffic right up until the early 1990s, including timber trains, as seen here at Kennethmont on 29 May 1990. Class 37 No. 37262 *Dounreay* approaches the former Great North of Scotland (GN of S) signal-box at Kennethmont with a morning Elgin–Aberdeen timber train.

Opposite, bottom: Having shunted the small goods yard at Huntly, Class 37 No. 37261 *Caithness* departs for Aberdeen at 8.30 a.m. with a pickup goods train from Elgin on 1 June 1990. Note the ScotRail symbol on the cab.

Above: After steam finished on the Waterloo–Exeter route in the mid-1960s, locomotive-hauled trains held sway until the early 1990s, when Class 159 units took charge. The popular English Electric Class 50s were in charge for several years, almost until the end of locomotive-hauled trains on this attractive route. Class 50 No. 50007 *Sir Edward Elgar* departs from London Waterloo on 27 April 1991 with the 11.15 service to Exeter. This locomotive was originally named *Hercules*, but was renamed and refurbished in GWR green and with classic style GWR cast numberplate in the early 1980s.

Opposite, top: At midday on Saturday 20 June 1981 at King's Cross station, we see Class 47/4 No. 47526 with an arrival from Leeds, while on its right is Deltic Class No. 55009 *Alycidon* which has just arrived with a train from York.

Opposite, bottom: By 1985, most of the trains from St Pancras to the East Midlands and Yorkshire were in the hands of the HST units. However, the Class 45s, from which the HSTs took over, could still be seen on postal trains, etc. On the evening of 25 March 1985, 'Peak' Class 45/1 No. 45122 is pictured under St Pancras' magnificent roof with the 10.25 postal train to Newcastle.

A Gloucester RC&W Co. single-car unit, No. W55019, waits at Penarth station to work the 12.05 shuttle service to Cadoxton on 8 July 1967. These Class 122 single units were first introduced in 1958, with seating for sixty-five second-class passengers. *(Hugh Ballantyne)*

The Pressed Steel Co. Class 121 single units were introduced in 1960. No. 55034 of that class is seen at Stoke Prior, south of Bromsgrove, on 30 May 1989 with the 10.41 Barnt Green–Worcester Foregate Street station service.

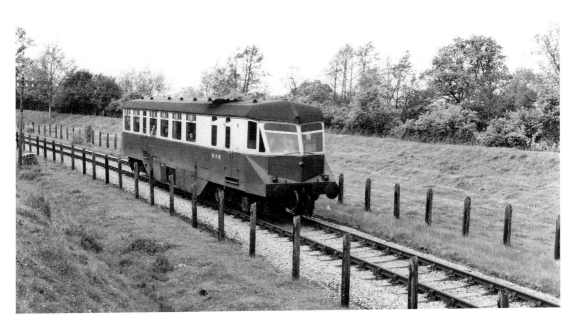

Former GWR (now Western Region) diesel railcar No. W19W of Gloucester shed (85B) is photographed on 11 May 1957 south of Barber's Bridge with the 12.05 Ledbury–Gloucester Central train. This unit was built at Swindon in 1940 but, along with the rest of the class, had been withdrawn by 1962. (*Hugh Ballantyne*)

German-built four-wheel railbus No. W79976 stands at Tetbury station on 7 February 1964 prior to working out with the 14.15 service to Kemble. The Tetbury–Kemble branch closed to passengers on 6 April 1964. (*Hugh Ballantyne*)

A 'Peak' on the Cornish main line with a mixed goods train. The location is the fine-looking eight-arch Lynher viaduct, some 5 miles to the west of Saltash. The train is a St Blazey–Tavistock Junction (Plymouth) freight, and the time is 10.30 a.m. on 29 May 1985. In charge is 'Peak' Class 45 No. 45056. In just over the hour that I was at this location, as well as the freight train I saw five locomotive-hauled passenger trains, with a Class 45, Class 47 and three Class 50 locomotives in charge. Those were the days!

At one time, passenger trains hauled by English Electric Class 37 locomotives could be found more or less all over the BR system, as these next two pictures demonstrate. The first picture, taken on 13 August 1988, shows No. 37411 *The Institute of Railway Signal Engineers* with the 14.15 Fort William–Mallaig train crossing over Loch nan Uamh viaduct.

The second view was taken on the Cambrian line from Shrewsbury to Pwllheli. The location is the boat yard at Frongoch (south of Barmouth). The train is the 16.56 (SO) Pwllheli–Euston service, hauled by Class 37/4 No. 37431 *Sir Powys/County of Powys* and the date is 16 June 1990. The Class 37s were first introduced in 1960, and were built between 1960 and 1965 by either English Electric at Vulcan Foundry, Newton-le-Willows, or by Robert Stephenson & Hawthorn at Darlington.

Class 37 No. 37227 approaches Clay Cross Junction on 22 February 1990 with a southbound mixed freight train bound for Derby and the West Midlands.

Still on 22 February 1990, only this time at Tupton, north of Clay Cross Junction. Class 58 No. 58041 heads north with an empty 'Merry-Go-Round' (MGR) train bound for the Sheffield area. The powerful Type 5 Class 58 locomotives were a fairly late arrival on the BR scene, being first introduced in 1983. They were also the first locomotives to appear in Railfreight grey livery.

This scene in the Clay Cross area shows Brush Type 5 Class 56 No. 56008 with a southbound MGR train near Tupton, also on 22 February 1990. These locomotives were first introduced in 1976 and built either in Romania or by British Rail Engineering Limited (BREL) at both Crewe and Doncaster Works.

The final picture in this Derbyshire quartet was taken many years earlier than the previous pictures – on 17 May 1966 – before the closure of the Midland Railway through route from St Pancras to Manchester. Brush Type 4 No. D1825 (later Class 47/3 No. 47344) leaves Millford Tunnel, north of Duffield, with a morning St Pancras–Manchester express via Millers Dale and Chinley.

At 6.15 p.m. on 5 August 1983, Class 37 No. 37019 leaves Ipswich tunnel and runs into Ipswich station with the 16.50 semi-fast train from Liverpool Street to Lowestoft. Note the split headcodes.

Some 45 minutes earlier than the previous scene, and we see Class 47/4 No. 47580 *County of Essex* approaching Ipswich station with the 16.20 from Liverpool Street to Norwich, 'The East Anglian'. At the time, this locomotive was shedded at Stratford TMD (London), hence the silver roof, a common sight on Stratford Class 47s.

For many years, the cross-country trains between Norwich and Birmingham New Street were in the hands of the Brush Type 2 Class 31 locomotives. Passing the Great Eastern signal-box at Thetford on 17 July 1983 is Class 31 No. 31184 with the 13.05 (SuO) Norwich–Birmingham train via March, Peterborough and Leicester. Note also the high repeater semaphore signals for sighting purposes.

These next two Deltic pictures were taken on 23 September 1978. In the upper view, we see immaculate No. 55019 *Royal Highland Fusilier* emerging from Stoke tunnel, south of Grantham, with the 15.00 King's Cross–Aberdeen train. Engineering work was in progress at the tunnel to lower the rail height, and the Down track was completely removed temporarily. *(Hugh Ballantyne)*

This picture shows Deltic No. 55008 *The Green Howards* at High Dyke, near Grantham, with the 10.55 King's Cross–Edinburgh train. *(Hugh Ballantyne)*

The following two scenes, both taken in 1966, show the famous Deltic locomotives in their original two-tone green livery, and with their earlier numbering. In this first picture, No. D9015 *Tulyar* hurries through the centre road at Wakefield Kirkgate station with an afternoon King's Cross–Leeds Central train on 19 September 1966.

The second view shows No. D9015 once again, this time in Leeds Central station after bringing in a morning train from King's Cross on 2 April 1966.

On 26 April 1984, Class 33 No. 33024 takes the LSWR route out of Exeter St David's station with an Up ballast train from Meldon quarry. The Exeter area had yet to be resignalled as can be seen from the array of semaphore signals and signal-box which are still visible.

Class 50 No. 50046 *Ajax*, having arrived at Newbury station with the 16.45 train from Paddington, is seen about to run around the empty train, which it will then take back to London as an empty coaching stock (ECS) working on 28 August 1985.

Framed by the former LNWR station at Rhyl, Class 37/4 No. 37417 *Highland Region* runs into the North Wales station with the 15.24 Crewe–Holyhead train on 1 September 1995.

Leicester London Road station on 9 July 1983 is the setting as 'Peak' Class 45 No. 45052 prepares to pull out of the station with the ECS of the 12.37 train from Skegness, the train itself having arrived at Leicester with Class 20s Nos 20183 and 20187 in charge. By now, the 'Peaks' had more or less finished on Midland main line passenger train duties and, as can be seen, could be found on a variety of different tasks.

The BRC&W Type 2 Class 26 locomotives were for many years to be seen on the Inverness–Wick and Thurso (Far North) route. On 20 August 1983, Nos 26024 and 26035 pull away from Dingwall, near the junction for the line to Kyle of Lochalsh, with the 11.40 train from Inverness to Wick and Thurso, the train dividing at Georgemas Junction. Note the fine-looking Highland Railway bracket signal with LMS attachments.

On the morning of 23 July 1988, Class 37/4 No. 37416 approaches the Kyle of Lochalsh with the 06.55 train from Inverness, having completed the 82☐ mile journey from the Highland capital in 2 hours 45 minutes, including thirteen possible station stops.

Our next location is Garve, some 30 miles from Inverness on the line to Kyle of Lochalsh. On Sunday 21 August 1983, Class 37 No. 37262 pulls out of the attractive HR station at Garve with the 09.30 Inverness–Kyle of Lochalsh train. On the right-hand side is the site of the former goods yard.

Above: Also on 13 May 1966, 'Peak' No. D113 approaches the summit of the Lickey Incline at Blackwell (around 2 miles of 1 in 37 from Bromsgrove to Blackwell) with a Bristol–Birmingham train.

Opposite, top: Type 4 'Peak' Class locomotive No. D25 hurrries along near Soulby, on the Settle & Carlisle line, with an afternoon Carlisle–Leeds train on 27 August 1967.

Opposite, bottom: On 13 May 1966, an unidentified 'Peak' Class locomotive is photographed south of Barnt Green station as it nears the top of the Lickey Incline with a morning Birmingham–Bristol train.

Class 47/4 No. 47604 departs
from Dalwhinnie station on the
afternoon of 30 July 1990 with
the 16.33 Inverness–Edinburgh
train. This station is located on the
1 in 80 climb up to Drumochter
Summit, which at 1,484ft above
sea level is the highest railway
summit in the British Isles. Note
also the HR station footbridge
and, on the right-hand side,
Dalwhinnie distillery.

The famous Cornish tented china clay wagons were replaced at about the end of 1987, and these next four views show them in the Lostwithiel and Par areas. Class 47 No. 47234 heads out of Lostwithiel station with a train of empty clay wagons on 27 April 1984. In a few yards, the train will reverse into the 'clay sidings' just off the Down platform.

On the evening of 28 August 1987, Class 37/5 No. 37671 *Tre Pol and Pen* approaches Par station with a clay train for St Blazey yard.

Class 37 No. 37181 leaves the sidings at Lostwithiel with a china clay train bound for Carne Point on the Fowey branch line on 27 April 1984.

This photgraph, taken on 24 August 1987, shows No. 37671 once again, this time passing the harbour at Golant (on the Fowey branch) with a train of clay wagons bound for Carne Point.

The beautiful station at York is bathed in late summer sunshine as a Down morning express prepares to depart for Edinburgh on 4 September 1988. This view shows the rear of the train, with HST No. 43047 *Rotherham Enterprise* in the attractive InterCity livery.

On 31 July 1987, an unidentified HST unit forming the 15.00 King's Cross–Edinburgh service crosses the Royal Border Bridge at Berwick-upon-Tweed and heads towards the capital city, with an arrival scheduled for 19.55, some 295 minutes for the 393☐ mile journey.

This third picture of HSTs on the ECML shows HST units, with No. 43110 leading, crossing Chester-le-Street viaduct with the 15.35 Edinburgh–King's Cross train on 11 August 1986.

A few months before the electrification of this area of the East Coast Main Line, HST unit with No. 43116 *City of Kingston upon Hull* leading and No. 43047 at the rear, rounds the curves at Penmanshiel, near Granthouse, with the 06.15 King's Cross–Edinburgh train on Saturday 1 August 1987.

The old engine house at Scorrier near Redruth in Cornwall has always been an attractive location for railway photographers, especially on 30 August 1984 when Class 50 No. 50007 *Sir Edward Elgar* hurries past the reminder of Cornwall's industrial heritage with the 16.35 Exeter–Plymouth–Penzance train.

The following day (31 August 1984) and we see Class 45 No. 45019 with a tank train from Tavistock Junction (Plymouth) to Ponsandane Depot (Penzance).

Class 25/2 No. 25239 approaches Appleby station on 30 September 1983 with a freight train for the Warcop branch line, which can be seen running to both the left- and right-hand sides of the Midland Railway signal-box. Although this former North Eastern line is now known as the Warcop branch, it used to run through to Kirkby Stephen (NE), and this section of the line from Appleby to Warcop was retained to service the army camp at Warcop.

On 3 January 1985, Class 25/3 No. 25300 enters Gobowen on the Shrewsbury–Chester line, with an empty stone train bound for Blodwell quarry, the line to which can be seen branching off on the right-hand side. Sister engine No. 25303 can just be seen to the left of the GWR signal-box with an Up stone train from Blodwell quarry. This was the final week of Class 25s working on these stone trains; they were replaced by Class 31s.

Plumpton Junction on the Carnforth–Barrow line is the location as Class 25/3 No. 25321 hurries by on 19 April 1984 with a Down nuclear flask train, bound for Sellafield.

This SR 'electric backwater' between Woodside and Selsdon was closed at the end of the 1982/3 timetable. Here a Class 416/2 two-car suburban unit (2-EPB), No. 5767, takes the points at the junction of the electrified and non-electrified lines at Selsdon, working as the 16.58 Sanderstead–Elmers End train on 15 April 1983. The Class 416/2 units were first introduced in 1953. *(Hugh Ballantyne)*

Class 207 East Sussex unit No. 1303 has just passed the LB&SCR signal-box as it departs from Eridge with the 12.31 train to London Bridge on 31 August 1983. These SR DEMUs were first introduced in 1962 and built at BR Eastleigh. Note also the fine early Southern Railway bracket signal.

Approaching Hove station on the afternoon of 30 August 1983 is Class 423 EMU No. 7728 with a Littlehampton train. These units were built between 1967 and 1974. Hove signal-box is an LB&SCR design, and the bracket signal is Southern Railway.

On 31 August 1983, Class 205 Hampshire unit No. 1107 enters Oxted station with an afternoon Eridge–London Bridge train. These three-car Class 205 DEMUs were built at Eastleigh Works in 1957.

Above: This view inside the maintenance depot at Plymouth Laira was taken on 3 April 1985, and shows English Electric Class 50 No. 50046 *Ajax* undergoing work. Note the (probably) experimental black livery on the locomotive's roof.

Opposite, top: This picture at Plymouth Laira was also taken on 3 April 1985 and shows Class 50 No. 50041 *Bulwark* outside the maintenance depot. These two Laira photographs were taken with the kind permission of BR.

Opposite, bottom: This view at BREL Doncaster Works was taken on 28 July 1984 and shows the powerful Class 58 diesels under construction. From left to right are Nos 58016, 58017 and 58018. *(Hugh Ballantyne)*

These next two pictures were taken at Stoke Prior, just south of Bromsgrove, on a very wintry 10 December 1990. The first scene, taken at 13.55, shows Toton-based Class 56 No. 56076 with a southbound train of empty mineral wagons. This locomotive was originally named *Blythe Power*, and was one of the batch Nos 56031–135 built at BREL at Doncaster or Crewe, Nos 56001–30 being built in Romania.

Some three-quarters of an hour later, and we see a pair of Class 37s, Nos 37719 and 37225, with a southbound train of mainly flat wagons.

On 2 April 1983, an unidentified Class 47 approaches Ais Gill summit (on the Settle–Carlisle route) with a diverted Plymouth–Glasgow train.

Class 45 No. 45064 enters Bescot station on 12 December 1983 with a southbound coal train from the Wolverhampton direction. The line to Walsall can be seen just to the right of the train, above which is the M6 motorway.

What must be a fairly rare picture is that of the Royal Train being hauled by a 'Western' Class diesel. This was certainly the case on glorious 1 June 1971, as No. D1045 *Western Viscount* is caught by the camera just west of Bathampton as it hauls the Royal Train conveying HRH Prince Philip from Westbury (Wiltshire) to Shirehampton (Bristol). *(Hugh Ballantyne)*

Class 37 No. 37142 runs light engine into Inverness station on 29 August 1986 in order to take out the 10.55 train to Kyle of Lochalsh. On the right of the picture is Inverness Rose Street signal-box, of Highland Railway design. With resignalling in the area shortly to take place, scenes like this soon disappeared. On the left-hand side is the 11.35 Inverness–Wick and Thurso train.

An afternoon northbound local DMU service passes the North British signal-box at the southern end of the Tay Bridge, and heads for Dundee (in the background) on 19 April 1981. This location, Wormit, was the junction for the line to Tayport and St Andrews, which was closed many years ago.

Craigo station on the Aberdeen–Dundee line closed in 1956 but this picture, taken on 2 August 1990, shows the Caledonian signal-box still in use, as Class 47/7 No. 47701 *Saint Andrew* hurries past with the 12.48 Aberdeen–Edinburgh train. No. 47701 was one of twelve Class 47s fitted for push-pull operation.

Smart-looking Class 37 No. 37251 approaches Nairn station on 22 August 1992 with the 12.15 Inverness–Aberdeen train.

On the afternoon of 9 April 1983, Class 47/4 No. 47443 pulls away from Hereford station with the return northbound 'Welsh Marches Pullman' (WMP) train from Newport to Shrewsbury. The southbound section was hauled by steam traction, with GWR 'Castle' 4–6–0 No. 5051 *Earl Bathurst* in charge from Shrewsbury to Hereford, and then on to Newport by SR 'King Arthur' 4–6–0 No. 777 *Sir Lamiel*.

The Crewe–Cardiff trains were until the mid-1980s mainly in the charge of Class 33 locomotives (see next picture). From then until the early 1990s, the Class 37s were mainly used on these services. Class 37/4 No. 37407 *Loch Long* (formerly of Eastfield Depot, Glasgow) approaches Sutton Bridge Junction, just south of Shrewsbury, with the 09.15 Liverpool–Cardiff train on 30 September 1989. Note the fine-looking GWR bracket signal, and the medieval Shrewsbury Abbey which dominates the background. The single track in the middle foreground (truncated behind the photographer) was the junction for the Severn Valley line to Bridgnorth and on to Worcester.

As stated in the previous caption, Class 33s dominated the Cardiff–Crewe workings until the mid-1980s, and on 4 January 1985 we see No. 33033 arriving at Ludlow station with the 11.45 from Cardiff to Crewe. These Type 3 locomotives are popularly known as 'Cromptons' because of their Crompton-Parkinson electrical equipment.

The western end of Newton Abbot station is the setting as Class 50 No. 50030 *Repulse* enters the outer Up platform with the 16.30 Plymouth–London Paddington train on 27 May 1984. Framing this scene is this fine example of a GWR gantry signal, complete with all its signals and finials. When this gantry was removed in the 1987 resignalling, it was purchased by the publishers David & Charles (the building on the left-hand side) and installed adjacent to their offices.

Class 47/4 No. 47419 runs through Cowley Bridge, north of Exeter St David's, with the 17.05 Plymouth–York train on Friday 29 July 1983. Cowley Bridge is the junction for the former SR route to Barnstaple and Okehampton.

In the summer of 1987, when there were still locomotive-hauled trains from Exeter to Barnstaple, Class 33 No. 33023 prepares to leave the former SR station at Barnstaple with the 13.53 train to Exeter on 26 September 1987. The station buildings have long gone, to be replaced by a 'bus shelter' with a single track.

On the morning of Monday 7 May 1985 (May Day bank holiday), 'Peak' Class 45 No. 45034 runs into Tiverton Junction station with an Up train of empty coal wagons. This station closed in May 1986, to be replaced by Tiverton Parkway station, which is situated about a mile north of this location.

Above: No scene at Chester would be complete without one of the magnificent LNWR signal-boxes that were to be seen in the station area. On 22 October 1983, Class 45/1 No. 45112 *The Royal Army Ordnance Corps* leaves Chester and runs underneath Chester No. 6 signal-box with the 13.39 Manchester Victoria–Bangor train.

Opposite, top: An Up goods from North Wales approaches the outskirts of the Roman city of Chester with Class 25/2 No. 25210 in charge. This location is called the Roodee, behind which is the famous Chester race course. The date is the early evening of Wednesday 13 July 1983.

Opposite, bottom: Turning around from the previous picture, and on the same day but a few minutes later, we see Class 47/4 No. 47540 emerging from the Chester 'Walls' and crossing over the Shropshire Union Canal at Northgate lock with the 17.34 Crewe–Holyhead train.

Above: No. 50033 *Glorious* in Network South East livery runs through the attractive countryside at Milborne (east of Sherborne) with the 16.15 Waterloo–Exeter train on 15 August 1991. It should also be pointed out that from about 1970 through to the introduction of the turbo units in 1993, the ubiquitous but less powerful Class 33s were regular performers on the line. (See picture on page 4.)

Opposite, top: The Southern Region (formerly LSWR/SR) main line from Waterloo to Exeter has undergone several changes over the years, including diesel traction. It would be fair to say that, after the end of steam on the line in 1965, the Warship Hydraulic locomotives were often to be found on this route until their withdrawal in the early 1970s. This picture shows 'Warship' Class No. D826 *Jupiter* speeding along the SR West of England line near Basing with a morning Waterloo–Exeter train on 2 July 1967.

Opposite, bottom: The diesel class that was to be seen on the Waterloo–Exeter line from 1980 to 1992 was the popular and powerful English Electric Class 50. No. 50046 *Ajax* in BR blue livery heads through North Perrott (east of Crewkerne) with the 13.15 Waterloo–Exeter service on 16 August 1991.

Class 47/4 No. 47407 makes an impressive start out of Edinburgh Waverley station with the 14.30 train to Glasgow Queen Street station on 30 March 1986. 45 minutes were allowed for the 47□ mile journey, including two stops, at Edinburgh Haymarket and Falkirk High stations, thus requiring some smart running between Scotland's two principal cities.

This picture at the east end of Edinburgh Waverley station was taken from above Calton tunnel on Wednesday 11 May 1983, and shows an unidentified Class 37 locomotive heading an Up tank train from Grangemouth Refinery. On the left-hand side can be seen a goods yard and solid looking signal-box, all of which disappeared with electrification in the late 1980s, and now most of the area is a car park.

This was the scene at Malmesbury on 12 June 1962 as 0–6–0 shunter No. D2187 shunts its daily goods train. Most of the traffic was agricultural machinery, some of which is awaiting loading on the (closed) station platform. Passenger traffic on the Dauntsey to Malmesbury branch ceased in 1951, but goods traffic survived until the end of 1962. The BR Class 03 shunting locomotives were introduced in 1959, and built at BR Swindon or Doncaster Works. *(Hugh Ballantyne)*

Class 20 No. 20066, Class 08 No. 08879 and Class 47/4 No. 47426 head north out of York station on 6 August 1986.

Exeter St David's station yard is the location as on 28 April 1984 Class 08 shunter No. 08840 waits to leave the sidings with an empty stock train. This area is also part of the diesel depot. The Class 08s were built between 1953 and 1962 by BR at Crewe, Darlington, Derby, Doncaster or Horwich Works. Note also the water crane, a remnant of when this area was also a steam shed – it closed to steam in 1964.

A wet evening at Carlisle station as Class 08 No. 08910 shunts empty stock, and electric locomotive Class 87 No. 87014 *Knight of the Thistle* prepares to leave with a northbound empty stock train on 29 January 1983.

Sunday 24 May 1992 was the final day of Class 50 haulage on the Waterloo–Exeter route. From that date, until the summer of 1993 when the Class 159 turbo units took charge on the line, the trains were in the hands of the Class 47 diesels. To mark the end of Class 50 haulage, two 'celebrity' locomotives, No. 50007 *Sir Edward Elgar* and D400 (formerly No. 50050 *Fearless*) were used. Also used on that day were Class 33s Nos 33002 and 33102. Nos D400 and 50007 are seen leaving Sherborne and climbing the 1 in 80 of Sherborne bank with the 15.43 Exeter–Waterloo train.

English Electric
Class 40 No. 40181
passes the former
LNWR Rhyl
No. 2 signal-box as
it pulls away from
Rhyl station on
6 July 1983 with the
11.35 Manchester
Victoria–Bangor
train (the 08.50
ex-Scarborough).

Another North Wales scene also on 6 July 1983, this time at Abergele. Class 40 No. 40047 heads east through the station with the 14.40 ex-Amlwch (Anglesey)–Manchester goods train. On the Down platform, a pair of Metropolitan-Cammell Class 101 units, with No. 51185 leading, wait to leave with the 14.44 Manchester Victoria–Llandudno local train.

Preparing to leave Appleby on 17 August 1983 is Class 40 No. 40122/D200 with the 10.40 Carlisle–Leeds train. Note that at this time No. 40122 was also numbered D200, the original numbering of the class being D200 to D399.

Class 40 No. 40035 pauses at Manchester Victoria station on 27 June 1984 with an eastbound stone train. Just visible on the side of the locomotive is the original name which adorned No. D235, *Apapa*. By the end of 1984, most of the class had been withdrawn from service.

It was rare to find a Class 50-hauled train on the Worcester–Stourbridge Junction–
Birmingham route. However, when Plymouth Argyle played against Watford in the FA
Cup semi-final at Villa Park on 14 April 1984, eleven special trains hauled by Class 50s
were run from Plymouth to Birmingham. Six ran via the Lickey Bank, and the other five
via Stourbridge Junction. This view shows No. 50046 *Ajax* running past Rood End sidings
at Langley (on the Stourbridge route) with one of the Plymouth–Witton (for Villa Park)
football excursions.

On a very wintry 25 January 1984, the 07.35 Plymouth–Birmingham New Street train runs by the Worcester & Birmingham Canal near Birmingham University with Class 50 No. 50017 *Royal Oak* in charge. The (then) new University station, which is situated just north of Birmingham Selly Oak, can be seen at the rear of the train.

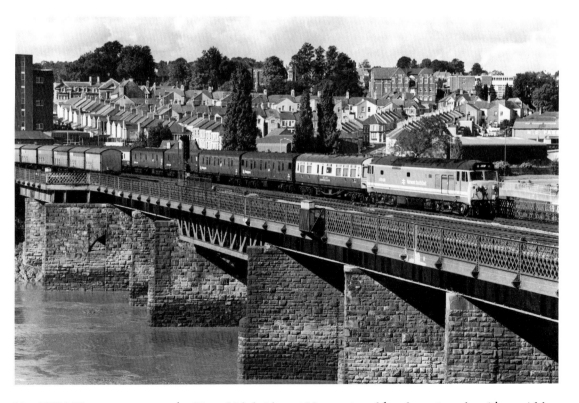

No. 50028 *Tiger* crosses over the River Usk bridge at Newport and heads eastwards with a midday parcels train on 25 September 1987. Note the leading vehicle is an inspection saloon.

The high North Eastern signal-box at Haltwhistle on the Carlisle–Newcastle line overlooks English Electric Class 37 No. 37106 as it trundles through Haltwhistle station on 15 August 1983 with a train of empty coal wagons bound for the Newcastle area.

This view at Haltwhistle (also taken on 15 August 1983) shows clearly the staggered platforms and fine-looking station footbridge, as well as the water crane. The outer platform was used for the branch line trains to Alston. This line closed in 1976, but happily on the trackbed of the line between Alston and Kirkhaugh is a miniature railway – the South Tyndale Railway. Leaving Haltwhistle is a Newcastle–Carlisle local train, comprised of a two-car Class 101 DMU.

On 6 June 1979, Class 46 No. 46035 passes under the North Eastern Railway signal-box at Hexham with the 09.12 Newcastle–Edinburgh train (diverted via Carlisle). The Class 46 locomotives were introduced in 1961 and were a final development of the 'Peak' Class 45 locomotives. Note also the high repeater signal on the left-hand side. *(Hugh Ballantyne)*

On the same day as the previous picture, Deltic Class No. 55009 *Alycidon* runs past the NER signal-box at Wylam with a diverted Newcastle–Edinburgh train. *(Hugh Ballantyne)*

Conversation piece at Exeter St David's station on 26 May 1984 – the driver of Class 50 No. 50030 *Repulse* exchanges a few words with the crossing keeper at the north end of St David's station, with the handsome looking GWR signal-box providing the background.

'Western' Class diesel No. D1026 *Western Centurion* waits to leave the carriage sidings at Paignton prior to taking out an Up passenger working on 22 July 1973.

Class 33 No. 33008 *Eastleigh*, complete with miniature snow ploughs, pauses at the eastern end of Newton Abbot station on 31 August 1985.

With St David's church in the background, 'Crompton' No. 33026 waits to enter Exeter St David's station on the afternoon of 11April 1983 in order to take out a local train to Paignton.

Above: On 16 June 1989, Class 56 No. 56033 approaches Fairwood Junction (Westbury) with a train of empty stone wagons bound for the quarries around Frome. On the right is the Westbury avoiding line, and in the background is the Westbury white horse.

Opposite, top: These next two scenes were taken at Westbury on Wednesday afternoon, 26 May 1983. In the first picture, a stone train has just arrived from the Frome area with Class 33 locomotives Nos 33106 and 33030 in charge, while on the outer tracks Class 37s Nos 37204 and 37241 are running light engine towards the Bristol line.

Opposite, bottom: The second scene, taken a few minutes later, shows Class 33 No. 33063 about to pass the GWR signal-box with the 13.10 Portsmouth–Bristol train. In both scenes there is an abundance of GWR semaphore signals.

Class 40 No. 40004 is photographed in the deep cutting approaching Chester No. 6 signal-box (see picture on p. 129) with the 09.37 Llandudno–Birmingham New Street train on 27 July 1979. (*Hugh Ballantyne*)

The English Electric Class 40 locomotives ran on the North Wales main line until the early 1980s. An unidentified member of this class, but believed to be No. 40020, approaches Chester General station with the 13.45 Manchester Victoria–Bangor train, and brightens up a very wet Saturday 5 June 1982.

By the 1990s, the Brush Type 2 Class 31 locomotives could often be found on Crewe–Holyhead trains. Looking very smart in InterCity livery, No. 31422 departs from Chester with the 14.53 Holyhead–Crewe train on a very sunny 15 August 1995.

Also to be seen on the North Wales route in the 1990s were the English Electric Type 3 Class 37s. Class 37/4 No. 37408 *Loch Rannoch* (formerly of Eastfield Depot, Glasgow, hence the Highland Terrier emblem) departs from Chester on 12 April 1997 with the 13.22 Bangor–Crewe train.

The Type 2 Sulzer Class 25 locomotives were something of a rarity in Scotland. However, on 3 October 1982, No. 25059 is photographed in the small goods yard at Blair Atholl station on the Perth–Inverness Highland Main Line. No. 25059 (D5209) is preserved on the Keighley & Worth Valley Railway.

Still on the Highland Main Line, this time at Dalwhinnie, south of Aviemore, Class 47/4 No. 47460 heads north on the afternoon of 30 July 1990 with the 14.40 Edinburgh–Inverness train.

Surrounded by a mass of semaphore signals, Class 37 No. 37261 shunts the empty stock of a Kyle of Lochalsh train at Inverness on 20 August 1983. The train will reverse back into the station to form the 10.45 Inverness–Kyle of Lochalsh train.

Class 37 No. D6997 passes through Magor on the South Wales main line west of Severn Tunnel Junction with an Up coal train on 26 May 1970. *(Hugh Ballantyne)*

On 20 July 1985 at Worcester Shrub Hill station yard, Class 37 No. 37224 shunts a fine-looking rake of empty wooden coal wagons. The rails in the foreground are part of the junction line to Hereford via Worcester Foregate Street station, the lines in front of the locomotive going to Droitwich and Birmingham.

This next picture is sadly a Somerset & Dorset Railway demolition scene. 'Hymek' No. D7031 is seen at Radstock on 29 December 1967 waiting to work southwards light engine to the railhead, while in the background, Class 08 No. D3185 shunts wagons onto the Western Region connection. *(Hugh Ballantyne)*

Preparing to leave the Somerset resort of Minehead is 'Hymek' Class No. D7026 with the 10.25 (SO) holiday train to Paddington on 18 July 1970. *(Hugh Ballantyne)*

Above: Class 33 No. 33021 enters Abergavenny station on 19 February 1983 with the 13.25 train from Crewe to Cardiff. Worthy of note are the platform canopies.

Opposite, top: With Class 08 No. 08686 looking on, Class 33 No. 33039 approaches Sutton Bridge Junction, just south of Shrewsbury, with the 10.03 Crewe–Cardiff Central train on 28 January 1984. On the right-hand side is the site of Shrewsbury locomotive shed (89A), and on the left by the 08 locomotive is the token catching equipment for the Cambrian route.

Opposite, bottom: The afternoon Crewe–Cardiff train hurries through Little Stretton (north of Church Stretton) on a misty 17 October 1981. In charge is Class 33/1 No. 33113, one of nineteen members of the class (Nos 33101 to 33119) that would shortly be fitted for push-pull working.

On 11 August 1990, Class 31 No. 31187 pulls away from Yarmouth station with the 10.40 (SO) train to Birmingham New Street. In the background waiting to leave on the 11.20 service to London Liverpool Street station is Class 47/4 No. 47584 *County of Suffolk*.

Passing under the famous signal gantry of Falsgrave Road, Scarborough, with the 08.35 (SuO) train from Bradford is Class 47 No. 47212. On the left-hand side is Class 08 shunter No. 08339. The date is Sunday 14 August 1983.

Within months of the electrification of the East Coast Main Line, Class 45 No. 45062 speeds along the four-track section at Avenue Grange near Thirsk with an Up train of flat wagons on 9 August 1986.

Having just crossed over the River Tyne at Newcastle via the King Edward Bridge, Class 47/4 No. 47544 then heads south to York with the 16.17 Newcastle–Liverpool cross-country service on 11 August 1986.

Above: In the summer service of 1990, the Manchester–Barrow-in-Furness trains were mainly in the hands of the Class 31 locomotives. On 26 July 1990, Class 31 No. 31400 pulls out of the picturesque station at Ulverston with the 13.18 Barrow–Manchester train. Ulverston is the birthplace of the great comedian Stan Laurel, and in 2009 a statue was unveiled, appropriately by Ken Dodd, at Ulverston of Stan Laurel and his equally famous partner Oliver Hardy.

Opposite, top: Class 47/4 No. 47594 runs through Poulton Junction station and approaches the outskirts of the world-famous seaside resort of Blackpool with the 10.40 London Euston–Blackpool train via Birmingham New Street, 17 September 1983. Giving the right of way to the train is a bracket signal dating from LMS days.

Opposite, bottom: Shunting under the wires at Carlisle station on 23 August 1983 is Class 40 No. D200 (also numbered No. 40122). The carriages would be from the 16.00 Leeds–Carlisle train, No. D200 being a regular locomotive on the Settle–Carlisle route.

Our final picture was also taken during the summer of 1990 (on 20 July), when Class 31s could also be found working on the Settle–Carlisle line. Class 31 No. 31416 runs through the Langcliffe Gorge (just north of Settle) with the 16.16 Carlisle–Leeds train.